Printed in the United States of America
First Printing, 2020
10 9 8 7 6 5 4 3 2 1
ISBN 978-0-578-58428-7

Lele Mai Publishing, LLC
18402 N. 19th Ave. #211
Phoenix, AZ 85023

Illustrator: Nancy Troupe

DEDICATION:
This book is dedicated to my granddaughter, Kali...
and all the children of the world.

ACKNOWLEDGEMENTS:
To my wonderful daughter Sydney Brown, thank you for your contribution!
To my brilliant and creative "A" team, whose understanding of my vision has brought this book to life; Nancy Troupe - Illustrator, Anna Weber - Literary Strategist, Ali Craig - Branding Expert and Project Manager, Linda Hollander - Sponsorship Expert, and Ryan Eisburg - Website Designer.

WOW! Look at the map they attached. Oh, my - this looks like a "big" construction project.

Then, when I get to the airport,
I say hi to my friends
who work there.

It feels good that we've
known each other for
a very long time.

And we're off!

Goodbye, Mrs. Airport
and kids!
See you when we
get back.

Be safe and have
a good flight, Mr. B.

Thanks, I'm sure we will.

HEY LOOK,
it's Ms. Hawk!

Good morning,
Ms. Hawk!

Well, hello, Mr. B,
how are you
today?

Our first stop is Downtown Phoenix, where we have a new high-rise building under construction.

Once we are finished
it's off to Sky Harbor Airport
where Mr. Sky Train
is being built.

It's off to Tucson we go,
Mr. Helicopter,

but first let's fly around the
west side of South Mountain --

I've been told there's something
beautiful to see!

THERE IT IS!

Just what I expected --
acres and acres of yellow desert wildflowers
blooming in the sunlight. How beautiful they look!

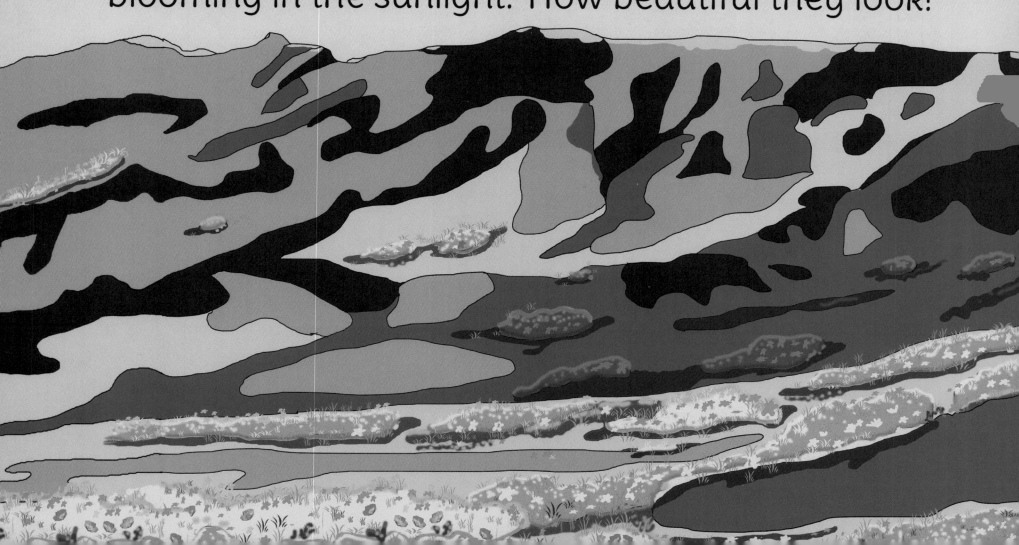

Hi, I'm the lead horse here, Mr. B.
We wanted to know where you are
going on this fine day.

We are off to Tucson, Mr. Horse.
You have a great day!

It's so beautiful up here!
Above the ground the air
is fresh and clean.
I love my office!

As we make our way, we can
see clouds start to form
patterns in the
sky.

It's amazing the shapes you can see in the clouds.
LOOK! There is a face!
And over there -- a giant bird!

It's great to see Tucson from way up here.
Now, let's look for the new construction site.

Fly down low, Mr. Helicopter
so I can take photos.

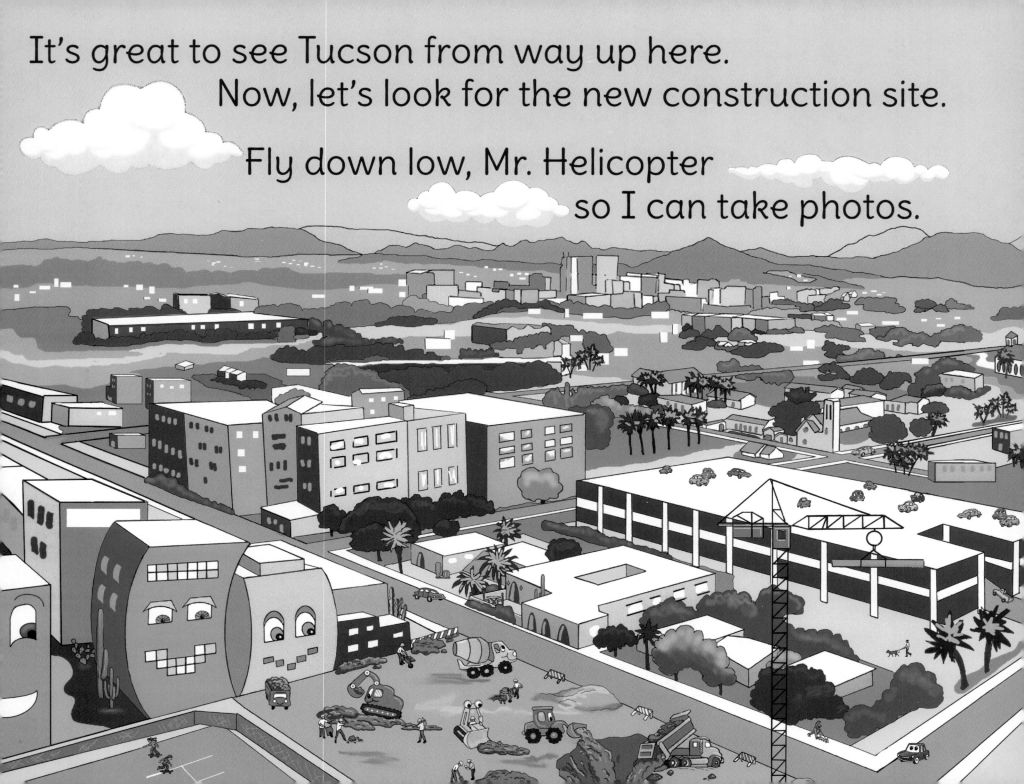

It sure looks like it's just a 'baby' project, Mr. B.
It shouldn't take long to take your pictures.

When you are done, we can head home.

This is my
favorite spot,
Mr. Helicopter.

Just look at those
Marching Saguaros.

They look like soldiers
marching up the mountainside.

OK, let's go home, Mr. Helicopter.

Yes. Let's do, Mr. B.
What a day we've had.

LOOK! The sun is starting to set.

It's so beautiful.
Aren't we lucky?

What a day!

Aerial photography,
helicopter office,
construction sites,
Arizona mountains
and valleys.

Kids,
remember to always
keep your head
in the clouds.

Mr. B.

CPSIA information can be obtained at www.ICGtesting.com
Printed in the USA
BVIW121122180220
572239BV00001BB/1